Hey, Where's My
Chicken Soup?

Hey, Where's My Chicken Soup?

Remembering the Unforgotten

Soul

of the

Preacher's Kid

RICHARD M. SALAZAR JR.

WINTERS
PUBLISHING GROUP

Published by Winters Publishing, LLC
2448 E. 81st St. Suite #4802 | Tulsa, Oklahoma 74137 USA

Book design copyright © 2014 by Winters Publishing, LLC. All rights reserved.
Cover design by Rodrigo Adolfo
Interior design by Caypeeline Casas

Published in the United States of America

ISBN: 978-1-63185-950-2
Religion / Christian Life / Spiritual Growth
14.07.08

Dedication

To our firstborn, Richard Matt Salazar III, who is six months old at the time of this writing. You too will one day read this book to find encouragement and added meaning for your life. Your mother and I have been given the awesome privilege of raising you to become all that God is calling you to be. May He endue you with power from on high the moment your time comes to take your rightful place to be used to radically transform your generation with power of the Holy Spirit!

Love,
Dad

I was blessed to be born one of the children of Billy and Ruth Graham. Being their child has without question brought to me a unique set of opportunities and challenges. I consider my parents people whom God has used in a remarkable way to advance the Gospel, and I have been privileged to enjoy a special relationship with both of them. But what is most important in every person's story is that God has a plan for each of His children. That makes every person very special—whether you happen to be a "preacher's kid" or not.

I believe that God sees us not as the child of a minister or missionary, but as an individual accountable to Him. It is my prayer that as you read the pages of this book, you will be inspired to yield yourself to the unique plan that God has just for you.

Franklin Graham
President & CEO
Samaritan's Purse
Billy Graham Evangelistic Association

Contents

A Note to My Readers

Although the title of my book suggests this project is for PKs only, this is certainly not the case! I wrote this book exclusively for the sons and daughters of all pastors, ministers, and missionaries. So if you fall into one of these three categories, then this is for you! However, as you read, you will only see references to PKs, and it will read as though this is the only audience I am writing to. I did this to save time and because I couldn't think of one word that would be all-inclusive. So wherever you see references to PKs, just drop your title in instead, and you will very quickly see how the ministry in this book will fit right into your world too!

I love you all dearly and pray God's best blessings and favor into everyone who reads this project!

Your friend,
Richard M. Salazar Jr.

Introduction

Theatrical sets can be magical, but seen from behind, the beautiful cascading fabric made to mimic water is simply a piece of cloth draped over some old cardboard boxes. Or the backdrop of a scenic mountain is nothing but a painted façade.

Families can be like this—beautiful on the outside, but false when viewed from another angle. And the families of pastors and spiritual leaders are especially susceptible. Even in the best families people can be a little crazy, a little off-base, a little over the edge. Dad has a bad day at work and comes home grumpy. Mom has had her hands full with a sick child, an uncooperative washing machine, or an overbearing boss. Add to the mix a car problem, a bad report card, and a burned dinner, and you have a recipe for the proverbial blow up. It happens—even in good families. This is normal.

But when your father is the pastor of the church and he gets up every Sunday to teach others about how to behave in accordance with Christian love, it can be difficult as a child to reconcile the sermon with the man who only yesterday hurled a wrench across the garage, barely missing the dog. As in all families, though, we survive such inconsistencies when grace and love are the bigger part of the equation. Love truly does cover a multitude of sins, and when practiced in the home, we soon learn to give grace and love to others, even our imperfect parents![1]

Unfortunately, not all ministers' homes are so grace-filled. In fact, there may be any host of "not normal" problems, and though children don't have the perspective that maturity brings to help us process those problems, they can certainly sense when something is very wrong, even if they can't verbalize it. And children are not blind. When they see one standard being preached through behavior at home, and another being preached through words from the pulpit, it registers.

Unfortunately, many ministers fall prey to the lie that they must "have it all together" in order to maintain their "expert" spiritual standing. Problems at home are, too often, a closely guarded secret, and discussing them outside the home is seen as a betrayal and possible threat to the family livelihood. In fact, sinful behavior may have even been spiritualized with language about authority or submission and obedience. Who are you, as the child, to question? If persistent problems were swept under the rug and a happy face employed to the world at large, you and your family never gained the perspective that strong, transparent friendships

---

[1] 1 Peter 4:8 "Above all, love each other deeply, because love covers over a multitude of sins." (NIV) *Holy Bible, New International Version* (Zondervan).

or even professional counseling offer. You may have even come to believe that abusive behavior is okay, as long as it is kept private.

Even in a healthy, loving minister's home the family is often subjected to a separate set of standards, even unintentionally, by the parents themselves or by the church or mission they serve. The pastor, his wife, and their children are simply not allowed to be human. No, they must live in some sort of Mount Olympus with all the other spiritual gods, never descending among mere mortals. As a result, preachers' kids may struggle with anger at the church or the mission for putting them and their family into a glass bubble. They may also struggle silently with hurts against themselves or their parents.

All children, but perhaps especially ministers' children, struggle between love for parents and other adult mentors and a growing awareness of their faults and frailties. It is difficult to see our parents or other church leaders as sinful humans, especially when they are so often lauded as spiritual heroes or bastions of the faith.

This book has been written with this maze in mind. It is a resource for you, the PK, to find encouragement, as well as a few "how to's" so you can be sane and effective in the role you live. As a PK you are not called to try and figure out how to escape your world, but instead, God wants to show you how to be a living giant in your world for years to come…starting now!

Identity

We have to be braver than we think we can be, because God is constantly calling us to be more than we are.

—Madeleine L'Engle

Identity is one of the hardest issues for a PK to understand. The reason why it's a difficult topic to understand is because identity is usually something that is chosen for you before you're able to grow into an identity you choose for your life. You're just kind of thrown into the role of a PK, and there really isn't much choice in the matter. And as hard as you try to become someone else, or even attempt to pursue what God is calling you to do in life, you are still…a PK! You can become the President of the United States, and yet all of your friends, family, and church members will still know you as…a PK! This can be frustrating to the point of annoyance, because you know deep down inside you have a growing desire to create your own identity, and yet, reality says you are nothing more than the son or daughter of a pastor.

Our enemy can use this to get you to believe that you have nothing to look forward to except living in the shadows of Mom and Dad for the rest of your life. By doing this he gets you to believe that you have no future, and ultimately can send you into a depression if you choose to listen to him. Increasing your self-awareness is about living authentically and overcoming your fears. Growing up, you may have been encouraged to conform or face the consequences. All PKs experience this. We live under the pressure of having to live what seems to be this perfect life, and we forget about what God is calling us to be.

> **"**
> Authentic living and self-awareness is
> about expressing honest thoughts, feelings,
> and opinions without feeling out of place.
> **"**

The best way to start thinking about your identity is to ask yourself some serious questions, such as:

- Who am I?
- Is there a pattern to my life?
- What direction is my life taking me in?
- What is my gift?
- What is my message?
- Is God confirming any of these in my life?

My point is this: you must make a decision to choose to conform to what God is asking you to be and do all you can to succeed. Authentic living and self-awareness is about expressing honest thoughts, feelings, and opinions without feeling out of place. It's called your identity!

As PKs we are probably the only group of people that has this craving of wanting to just blend in with the crowd. Well, the good news is you can live a normal life just like everyone else despite your position as a PK. In fact, finding your true identity and being yourself is the greatest gift you can give to your family, friends, and the world.

Here are four basic foundational bricks you can lay in your life, starting right now, to locate your identity and begin living in it:

#1 Take risks.

Allow yourself to be vulnerable by trying new things in life. If you're afraid, find creative solutions to your fears. This will help you to find your true identity and strengthen your self-esteem.

#2 Express your inner emotions.

If you're sad, let yourself feel sad and cry. Finding your true identity means staying in touch with your true emotions. Expressing yourself will increase your self-esteem, strengthening self-confidence and revealing your authentic self.

#3 Stay in touch with your dreams and goals.

All of us have responsibilities and pressures in life as a PK, but these responsibilities should not keep you from finding your true identity. Even if you can't actively work toward pursuing a profession or ministry or writing a book or going back to school, you can still envision yourself achieving your goals some day.

#4 Listen to your gut.

This really means to listen to your inner spirit. What is God saying to you? To find your authentic self, put other people's expectations aside. What do you think, feel, and want? One way to find your true identity and honor self-improvement is to know you care what others think... and listening to your gut anyway. You can care what people think and still find yourself—and be your authentic self. Listening to your gut helps with honoring your self-development, strengthening self-esteem, and finding your true identity.

Resource from the Source

> I will instruct you and teach you in the way which you should go; I will counsel you with My eye upon you.
>
> Psalm 32:8 (NASB)

You will show me the path of life; in Your presence is fullness of joy, at Your right hand there are pleasures forevermore.

Psalm 16:11 (NASB)

Trust in the LORD with all your heart
And do not lean on your own understanding.
In all your ways acknowledge Him,
And He will make your paths straight.

Proverbs 3:5-6 (NASB)

But if any of you lacks wisdom, let him ask of God, who gives to all generously and without reproach, and it will be given to him. But he must ask in faith without any doubting, for the one who doubts is like the surf of the sea, driven and tossed by the wind.

James 1:5-6 (NASB)

For this reason also, since the day we heard of it, we have not ceased to pray for you and to ask that you may be filled with the knowledge of His will in all spiritual wisdom and understanding…

Colossians 1:9 (NASB)

Feeding Your Inner PK

> Committing yourself is a way of finding out who you are. A man finds his identity by identifying.
>
> —Anonymous

> An identity would seem to be arrived at by the way in which the person faces and uses his experience.
>
> —James Baldwin

> Most people are other people. Their thoughts are someone else's opinions, their lives a mimicry, their passions a quotation.
>
> —Oscar Wilde

> We know what we are, but not what we may be.
>
> —William Shakespeare

> We have to be braver than we think we can be, because God is constantly calling us to be more than we are.
>
> —Madeleine L'Engle

> Define yourself radically as one beloved by God. This is the true self. Every other identity is illusion.
>
> —Brennan Manning

Journal

Do I know who I am as a person and as a child of God? If not, why?

_____

_____

_____

_____

_____

_____

_____

_____

_____

_____

Am I allowing others around me to frame who I am? If so, who might these people be, and why am I letting them?

_____

_____

_____

_____

_____

_____

_____

_____

_____

What does God's Word tell me about my identity as a person and as His son or daughter?

_____

_____

_____

_____

_____

_____

_____

_____

_____

How do I see myself right now and how does that align with what God says about me?

_____

_____

_____

_____

_____

_____

_____

_____

_____

What steps can I take right now to begin the process of living in my purpose?

_____

_____

_____

_____

_____

_____

_____

_____

_____

Faith

The Christian does not think God will love us because we are good, but that God will make us good because He loves us.

—C.S. Lewis

The faith of a PK is very special. The fact that there are still sons and daughters of pastors, ministers, and missionaries serving the Lord is an awesome thought. To go through what we go through, or went through, and yet still remain faithful to the Lord is astounding! This tells me that although the enemy tries his best to ruin the home of pastors, there are still those who are fighting against the strategies of the devil and winning. This is the key—winning. The goal is to win against the devil. And the best way to win is to choose to serve the Lord no matter what comes our way to shake our faith.

On the other hand, there are PKs who have lost the battle or right now are losing the continuous struggle to do what is right. Their faith walk is weakened day after day because of their inability to fight the good fight of faith! But that is okay, because we are here for them. Maybe you are one of those who are finding it difficult to win against the daily attacks on your faith. Please listen to me clearly… You can win! God is on your side always! Your faith is the reason why you are still breathing. You are reading this book because God loves you and because of your position in Christ—you will win!

> **"**
>
> God loves you, and He is on your side!
>
> **"**

If you are going to serve God to the best of your ability, certainly you need to know Him and His Word. That's why Bible study, prayer and fellowship are so important. Studying His Word, meditating on His person, and sharing in prayer and fellowship with His people help you to know and apply His will in your life.

Many PKs abandon their relationship with God and leave the faith for a number of different reasons, but this should not influence you or give you great reason to follow along. Indeed, you probably have valid reasons for why you should walk away from the Lord, but sin is sin, no matter who we are.

Satan can't deny the fact that you're serving the Lord, but he'll challenge your reason for doing it! Listen to this conversation between God and the devil from Job 1:8-9 (NLT):

God says, "Have you noticed my servant Job? He is the finest man in all the earth."

Satan replied, "Not without good reason! You have always protected him and his home and his property. You have made him prosperous in everything he does. Take away everything he has, and he will surely curse you to your face!"

And how does the chapter end?

"In all of this, Job did not sin by blaming God" (Job 1:22, NLT).

You see, when it comes to faith, everyone is on the same playing field, and the blessings or consequences, depending on the decisions we make, will come to all of us. Position and title have nothing to do with it. Yes, I believe it is a bit more difficult for all PKs to live a stable and healthy relationship with God, but the blessings of choosing to fight the good fight are real and available to you too!

God loves you, and He is on your side! Now, I can do one of two things in this section. I can give you a list that is as long as Highway 10 of all the reasons why PKs just like you abandon their faith, or I can give you solid reasons why you should grow closer with the Lord. I will do the latter. It does you or me no good to list out all of the reasons why PKs give up, because that doesn't help encourage you to keep going. What will motivate you is to show you what God does for those who remain faithful to him and how much better life can be when you do!

Here are four powerful motivators for maintaining your relationship with God:

#1 Love

This includes first a love for God, then an accompanying love for others. Love for God would also mean love for that which God loves, His people. We love other people.

#2 Gratitude

The best way to show our gratitude to God is by our service. Our lives become a thank you to Him. In light of God's blessings, we are motivated to offer our bodies to Him and to live for Him.

#3 Blessings Here and Then

We can also be motivated by God-given rewards in this life and in eternity. The judgment seat of Christ is the scene of future rewards. Eternal rewards include treasures and crowns. We also have a promise of earthly rewards. These come in the form of success—success in your finances, career, health, business, etc. Rewards are not a selfish motivation if our goal is to use them to glorify God in the end.

#4 Duty/Purpose

Christians serve God because they have made a commitment to do so or because they are living up to that which God has called them to do. Duty does not expect a reward but is performed out of obligation. Another form of duty would be purpose. Christians might also feel it their duty to be faithful stewards of their purpose. This is where the earthly rewards kick in!

Resource from the Source

> You who sit down in the High God's presence,
>   spend the night in Shaddai's shadow,
> Say this: "God, you're my refuge.
> I trust in you and I'm safe!"
> That's right—he rescues you from hidden traps,
> shields you from deadly hazards.
> His huge outstretched arms protect you—
> under them you're perfectly safe;
> his arms fend off all harm.
> Fear nothing—not wild wolves in the night,
> not flying arrows in the day,
> Not disease that prowls through the darkness,
> not disaster that erupts at high noon.
> Even though others succumb all around,
> drop like flies right and left,
> no harm will even graze you.
> You'll stand untouched, watch it all from a distance,
> watch the wicked turn into corpses.
> Yes, because God's your refuge,
> the High God your very own home,
> Evil can't get close to you,

harm can't get through the door.
He ordered his angels
to guard you wherever you go.
If you stumble, they'll catch you;
their job is to keep you from falling.
You'll walk unharmed among lions and snakes,
and kick young lions and serpents from the path."

Psalm 91:1 (The Message)

But now that you've found you don't have to listen to sin tell you what to do, and have discovered the delight of listening to God telling you, what a surprise! A whole, healed, put-together life right now, with more and more of life on the way! Work hard for sin your whole life and your pension is death. But God's gift is real life, eternal life, delivered by Jesus, our Master.

Romans 6:23 (The Message)

If we confess our sins, He is faithful and righteous to forgive us our sins and to cleanse us from all unrighteousness.

1 John 1:9 (NASB)

This is how much God loved the world: He gave his Son, his one and only Son. And this is why: so that no one need be destroyed; by believing in him, anyone can have a whole and lasting life. God didn't go to all the trouble of sending his Son merely to point an accusing finger, telling the world how bad it was. He came to help, to put the world right again. Anyone who trusts in him is acquitted; anyone who refuses to trust him has long since been under the death sentence without knowing it. And why? Because of that person's failure to believe in the one-of-a-kind Son of God when introduced to him.

John 3:17 (The Message)

Feeding Your Inner PK

I came all this way for a reason. Today is the day of salvation. Trust Jesus to save you. Then be sincere, as God knows a pretender.

—Kirk Cameron

My salvation was a free gift. I didn't have to work for it and it's better than any gold medal that I've ever won.

—Betty Cuthbert

The Bible is one of the greatest blessings bestowed by God on the children of men. It has God for its author; salvation for its end, and truth without any mixture for its matter. It is all pure.

—John Locke

There is but one Church in which men find salvation, just as outside the ark of Noah it was not possible for anyone to be saved.

—Thomas Aquinas

Journal

Have I kept the faith? Why or why not?

_____

_____

_____

_____

_____

_____

_____

_____

_____

_____

Do I know God loves me and am I able to love others?

_____

_____

_____

_____

_____

_____

_____

_____

_____

What can I do or what am I already doing to serve God?

_____

_____

_____

_____

_____

_____

_____

_____

_____

_____

Are there other PKs I can reach out to who are struggling
with their faith?

_____

_____

_____

_____

_____

_____

_____

_____

_____

_____

Are there other PKs I can be encouraged by who are keeping the faith?

_____

_____

_____

_____

_____

_____

_____

_____

_____

What scriptures in God's Word encourage me to stay the course?

_____

_____

_____

_____

_____

_____

_____

_____

_____

My prayer to God to persevere in the faith:

_____

_____

_____

_____

_____

_____

_____

_____

_____

_____

Success

Our greatest glory is not in never failing, but in rising up every time we fail.

—Ralph Waldo Emerson

Has it ever seemed as though PKs are the last ones to find out that they too can pursue their dreams just like anyone else? If you are a PK, you may feel like you are taking a giant leap off a cliff to even consider pursuing your God-given dreams. Sometimes, there is a great deal of pressure to follow in the ministry steps of our parents—to become a pastor or go into some other kind of full-time ministry role.

But God gives each of us unique gifts, dreams, and desires, and sometimes we have to give ourselves permission to chase those dreams down—even if they take us down a very different path from our parents. For some, the dream may indeed be a call to go to ministry; for others, it could be any number of other directions: legal, medical, creative careers, culinary—even entrepreneurial. Opportunities are endless, yet the thought of pursuing a profession outside of the ministry can be chilling, especially if you've been pressured, directly or indirectly, in that direction. After all, the only opportunities we are often exposed to on a regular basis are ministry-related, so we may be prone to believe that ministry will be our lifelong career simply because it is what we know.

However, ministry could prove disastrous to us if our passions and gifts simply are not well placed there. At the same time, we could be missing out on opportunities to put those passions and gifts to work where they are needed most.

I am reminded of my friend Brent, a PK from Texas. One of his biggest concerns as a young adult was his lack of ability to make it in a profession outside of ministry. He told me he had always wanted to be a stockbroker. One day he worked up the courage, shortly after graduating from seminary, to break the news to his parents that he had decided to not go into the ministry full-time but to pursue a career in the financial industry. He believed with everything in him that it was the right thing to do, but his natural mind was calling him a fool! Brent was so afraid of venturing out into new territory that he believed he would never make it as a financial advisor and that he really should take another look at ministry because, after all, it is what he was raised in. But Brent decided to go for his dream. With God's help, and a little encouragement from those who believed in Brent, he did choose to be a stockbroker and after fifteen years has become one of the most successful stockbrokers in the Southwest.

Brent had a difficult decision to make, but he found the courage to chase after his dream, and he won! What is your dream? What do you feel God is challenging you to do— even if others think you are insane? God believes in you. He gave you the dream, and it's up to you to go and get it!

Let me clarify my thought. Although most people experience a certain element of success in their career paths, this does not mean that they are in God's perfect will. I believe career paths, including lifelong goals, should be chosen and aligned according to God's purpose for our lives. It does us no good to be successful at something God is not calling us to do. It is important for us to learn, especially during our younger years, that our life should be planned according to what God has purposed us to do. We have heard a lot in recent years about purpose as it relates to life. There is nothing worse than to find out later in life that you have spent years working hard at something God really did not have in mind for you. Learn now, if you haven't already, to know what it is God is asking you to do at this season in your life, and then pursue it. Follow the leading of the Holy Spirit—He is given to us to guide us into all God has for us!

Having said this, it is possible that we can go too far in over spiritualizing our career path search. We are waiting for a "word from the Lord" or for some kind of dream or random Scripture to point us in the right direction—as though we are looking to some sort of spiritual Ouija board for answers. Instead, we should pay attention to what is already happening in and around us. How is God already speaking to you?

- Which activities do you do that cause you to lose track of time altogether? Is it organizing things? Writing? Drama? Building things? Do you lose all track of time when you are helping friends work through their problems? Whatever it is, when you find that time has passed without you even noticing, you are likely engaged in using your God-given gifts—and it makes sense to pursue a line of work that allows you to develop and use those gifts to the full.

- What do your friends say about you? If they are always telling you what a great speaker you are, maybe you should consider developing those skills. Could there be a future career in communications for you? Are you called to be a minister? Keep all the cards on the table, and trust God to lead you.

- Where are your present opportunities? Maybe you have a gift for building things and you have a present opportunity to work with a local builder. Does that mean you'll do that for the rest of your life? Probably not. Most people will go through multiple career changes in their lifetime. The days when we worked for one company our whole lives is long gone. So if your ultimate goal is to own your own interior design firm one day, but you're working in a restaurant to pay the bills right now—don't sweat it. Take advantage of the opportunities right in front of your nose. Can you put your design skills to work by freshening the tables with flowers and paying extra attention to place settings? Can you look for opportunities at home or among friends to use your gifts to delight others? You'll be amazed at how doing so develops your gifts and enriches those around you. You'll also find that new opportunities will arise if you keep your eyes open. Before you know it, you could be designing special events for friends and, voilà! You've soon launched a small business. Persistently using your gifts to serve with excellence is one of the best ways to insure more opportunities will come your way.

> **"**
> Life always presents challenges
> and setbacks, but don't let those
> discourage you from pursuing
> what God has placed in your heart. **"**

Whatever you decide to do, beware of allowing fear to creep in and trip you up. For instance, you may decide that ministry is, indeed, in your future, but you may feel called to work in a completely different manner, tradition, even a different denomination than the one in which you were raised. I won't lie—those decisions are not easy, and the fall-out can be anywhere from non-existent to severe, depending on the relationships and personalities of your family. But part of growing up is making your own decisions and taking full responsibility for them. And guess what? You won't always get it right. The arguments your parents may make against your decisions may sometimes be right and sometimes wrong—whether the advice is delivered gently or not. But remember this: your decisions are yours to live with. You have to make some mistakes in order to learn. You have to step out in the direction God is leading even to learn to hear God's voice. Living, making choices, and learning from them are all necessary components of learning the difference between God's voice and your own.

It is comforting to know, though, that God is bigger than all of our mistakes, so we can never blow it so badly that we have stepped outside the edge of God's mercy. It's also comforting to know that if we really seek direction and wisdom from God, He promises to give us the direction and wisdom we need. That's a promise. And it provides a solid foundation for us to step out and try things. God's grace is our touchstone and safety net.

When children are just learning to walk, the parents are always close at hand so that the child, who is guaranteed to fall, doesn't do any permanent damage! Parents will remove sharp-cornered tables, or they will hold onto one tiny hand to guide, or they will even provide "walkers" to give the child safe walking practice. God is like that with us. The Scriptures say that He leads us with "cords of kindness" just like a mother might hold onto a child's hand (Hosea 11:4). God knows we're going to fall, bruise our heads, scrape our knees, cry, and make a fuss. But it's all part of learning to walk. And it's all okay. He's right there to pick us up, dust us off, assure us we are still alive and well, and send us back to try again—knowing all the while that the same scenario will happen many times over before we learn to walk.

Ultimately, we need to listen closely to the Lord and follow the desires He has placed inside of us. It won't always be easy. Life always presents challenges and setbacks, but don't let those discourage you from pursuing what God has placed in your heart. After all, God gives us dreams and passions, much like a gift is given to us at Christmas or on our birthdays. God chooses dreams just for you to enjoy— so go and enjoy them!

Resource from the Source

For I know the plans that I have for you," declares the LORD, "plans for welfare and not for calamity to give you a future and a hope."

Jeremiah 29:11

"Ask and it will be given to you;" He said, "Seek and you will find; knock and the door will be opened to you. For everyone who asks receives; he who seeks finds; and to him who knocks, the door will be opened."

Matthew 7:7-9

There is surely a future hope for you, and your hope will not be cut off.

Proverbs 23:18

Against all hope, Abraham in hope believed and so became the father of many nations.

Romans 4:18

Feeding Your Inner PK

Dream as if you'll live forever, live as if you'll die today.

—James Dean

The only thing that will stop you from reaching your dreams is you.

—Tom Bradley

Don't be pushed by your problems, be led by your dreams.

—Anonymous

Follow your dreams, for as you dream you shall become.

—Anonymous

Yesterday is but today's memory, tomorrow is today's dream.

—Kahlil Gibran

Vision without action is merely a dream. Action without vision just passes the time. Vision with action can change the world.

—Joel Barker

Your dreams come true when you act to turn them into realities.

—Anonymous

It may be that those who do most, dream most.

—Stephen Butler Leacock

Journal

What is my definition of being successful?

_____

_____

_____

_____

_____

_____

_____

_____

_____

Do I consider myself successful both in life and in my relationship with God? If not, why not?

_____

_____

_____

_____

_____

_____

_____

_____

_____

_____

What areas of my life are lacking success?

_____

_____

_____

_____

_____

_____

_____

_____

_____

_____

What promises are found in God's Word for my life?

_____

_____

_____

_____

_____

_____

_____

_____

_____

_____

What steps can I take right now toward being a success?

_____

_____

_____

_____

_____

_____

_____

_____

_____

My prayer for success:

_____

_____

_____

_____

_____

_____

_____

_____

_____

_____

Criticism

Do what you feel in your heart to be right—for you'll be criticized anyway.

—Eleanor Roosevelt

Okay, here is a topic that every reader of this book will experience. In fact, you probably have already, without a doubt, and I'm sure in a very big way! It's all part of the position. Criticism is to be expected a hundred times over for the pastor and his family. Of course it is unfair, but it just comes with the territory. It is inevitable that criticism will be part of your daily life. If there is any good news from this, it's the fact that you are only one out of millions of other PKs around the world who experience constant criticism that, most of the time, is either unfair, unjust, or just plain old out of line. Statistics continually show that church members are always looking to criticize the pastor and his family, and the stats also show that church members expect the pastor's kids to live above the average standards for the rest of the church. Talk about unfair!

I wish there was some miracle trick that would minimize the pain we feel when being criticized, but unfortunately, these are hurts that we feel for long periods of time.

The good news to this is that we do not have to feel this pain alone. God is right there with us, he and saw the criticism coming before we did and is ready to bring comfort and joy immediately after we feel the pain.

However, I think it is relatively important to say that some criticism is necessary. The best way to view those critics is to see them as God speaking to us directly. There is nothing wrong with taking the criticism and aligning them with God's standards to see if the criticisms are valid. After all, we are human just like our critics, and we too are vulnerable to compromise.

Here are five ways to handle criticism wisely:

#1 Take immediate control of your initial reaction.

If your first reaction is to lash back at the person giving the criticism or to become defensive, take a minute before reacting at all. Take a deep breath, and give it a little thought.

#2 Thank the critic.

Even if someone is harsh and rude, thank them. They might have been having a bad day, or maybe they're just a negative person in general. But even so, your attitude of gratitude will probably catch them off-guard.

#3 Evaluate and learn.

After seeing criticism in a positive light and thanking the critic, don't just move on and go back to business as usual. Actually try to improve.

That's a difficult concept for some people, because they often think that they're right no matter what. But no one is always right. You, in fact, may be wrong, and the critic may be right. So see if there's something you can change to make yourself better.

#4 Turn a negative into a positive.

Find the positive in criticism. Sure, it may be rude and mean, but in most criticism you can find a nugget of gold: honest feedback and a suggestion for improvement.

#5 Be the better person.

Too many times we take criticism as a personal attack, as an insult to who we are. But it's not. Well, perhaps sometimes it is, but we don't have to take it that way. Take it as a criticism of your actions, not your person. If you do that, you can detach yourself from the criticism emotionally and see what should be done. By attacking the attacker, you are stooping to his level. Even if the person was mean or rude, you don't have to be the same way. You don't have to commit the same sins.

If you can rise above the petty insults and attacks and respond in a calm and positive manner to the meat of the criticism, you will be the better person. How do you stay above the attacks and be the better person? You rise above by removing yourself from the criticism and looking only at the actions criticized, by seeing the positive in the criticism and trying to improve, by thanking the critic, and by responding with a positive attitude.

> **"**
> If you can rise above the petty insults and attacks and respond in a calm and positive manner to the meat of the criticism, you will be the better person. **"**

Resource from the Source

If you reason with an arrogant cynic, you'll get slapped in the face;
confront bad behavior and get a kick in the shins.
So don't waste your time on a scoffer;
all you'll get for your pains is abuse.
But if you correct those who care about life,
that's different—they'll love you for it!
Save your breath for the wise—they'll be wiser for it;
tell good people what you know—they'll profit from it.

Skilled living gets its start in the Fear-of-God,
insight into life from knowing a Holy God.
It's through me, Lady Wisdom, that your life
  deepens,
and the years of your life ripen.
Live wisely and wisdom will permeate your life;
mock life and life will mock you.

Proverbs 9:9-10 (Message)

Intelligent children listen to their parents; foolish
children do their own thing.

Proverbs 13:1 (Message)

Refuse discipline and end up homeless;
embrace correction and live an honored life.

Proverbs 13:18 (Message)

Consider Jesus' example:

And while being reviled, He did not revile in return;
while suffering, He uttered no threats, but kept
entrusting Himself to Him who judges righteously.

1 Peter 2:23 (NASB)

Feeding Your Inner PK

If you are not criticized, you may not be doing much.

—Donald H. Rumsfeld

To avoid criticism do nothing, say nothing, be nothing.

—Elbert Hubbard

Criticism may not be agreeable, but it is necessary. It fulfills the same function as pain in the human body. It calls attention to an unhealthy state of things.

—Winston Churchill

We need very strong ears to hear ourselves judged frankly, and because there are few who can endure frank criticism without being stung by it, those who venture to criticize us perform a remarkable act of friendship.

—Michel de Montaigne

If you have no critics you'll likely have no success.

—Malcolm X

I find that the very things that I get criticized for, which is usually being different and just doing my own thing and just being original, is the very thing that's making me successful.

—Shania Twain

Journal

How do I generally handle criticism?

_____

_____

_____

_____

_____

_____

_____

_____

_____

_____

Do I generally separate the criticism from the critic? Why or why not?

_____

_____

_____

_____

_____

_____

_____

_____

_____

What are some proactive ways I can handle criticism and critics in the future?

_____

_____

_____

_____

_____

_____

_____

_____

_____

_____

What is some constructive criticism I've received, and have I benefitted from it?

_____

_____

_____

_____

_____

_____

_____

_____

_____

_____

What has God shown me through receiving criticism the right way?

_____

_____

_____

_____

_____

_____

_____

_____

My prayer to God to be gracious and teachable when receiving criticism:

_____

_____

_____

_____

_____

_____

_____

_____

_____

Trust

Love and trust, in the space between what's said and what's heard in our life, can make all the difference in the world.

—Fred Rogers

Trust is a huge issue for PKs. We trust no one! And it's not because we want to be arrogant. It takes a lot of effort to be arrogant. Nobody chooses to be arrogant unless they have worked at it for a long period of time. PKs don't have that kind of time nor do we live in an atmosphere that encourages arrogance. The reason why we have a hard time trusting is because we have been let down by others personally, or we have experienced being disappointed or betrayed as a family by people in the church. These kinds of experiences will naturally cause us to not trust people—we don't trust Christians, and we don't trust sinners.

I know that you're hoping that I will endorse a distrusting attitude since I have struggled with it, and it seems to be a valid way of thinking and living considering the continuous betrayal we experience by people around us. Well, as much as I understand the reasoning, I absolutely cannot endorse the idea that we can live without trusting others.

Distrust is supposed to work for our protection, but there's an inherent problem with distrust when it works overtime: every human heart wants and needs intimacy, but distrust puts genuine intimacy out of reach.

Distrust is today's most deadly epidemic. When you're considering any significant human involvement, your friends probably warn you to be careful—reminding you, in so many words, that you should be suspicious and distrustful.

When we distrust people, we are choosing to drive ourselves into the shadows of self-defeating alienation. How can you learn to trust people when you are routinely assuming everyone is out to hurt you? PKs live in a world where the chances of being hurt are much higher than the average church member, *but* you must find a way to learn how to trust people again. Learn how to find those one or two people in your life who can be trusted so you can find hope and healing whenever you need it.

Here are three easy ways you can learn how to develop trust once again:

#1 Get rid of your expectations.

The scars of being hurt in the past are real. I understand this. But you cannot let scars from the past keep you from moving forward. If you expect to get hurt, you will get hurt. You *must* take your doubt in others and your scars and leave them at the feet of Jesus. Ask Him to bring right relationships into your life, and you will be surprised at how He quickly moves to make it happen!

#2 Establish clear boundaries.

Set up boundaries that might allow you to feel more trusting. A boundary is a limit or edge that defines you as separate from others. You have a limit to what is safe and appropriate. You have a border. Within this border is you—that which makes you an individual different and separate from others. You're not married to your trusted friends, so there needs to be an understanding of what you are looking for in a friendship. Those who genuinely love you will understand your expectations by being there for you without ultimatums.

#3 Trust yourself.

Unless trusted friends give you a real reason to mistrust or doubt their honesty, you must learn to trust in them. Never accuse your trusted relationships unless you have hard evidence. Without proof you'll just create an air of mistrust. Trust your judgment. Know that you have done everything right in choosing your trusted friends. Live with confidence, knowing that God has brought great people into your life to help you.

"

> When we distrust people, we are
> choosing to drive ourselves into the
> shadows of self-defeating alienation.

"

Resource from the Source

Friends come and friends go, but a true friend sticks
by you like family.

Proverbs 18:24 (Message)

Become wise by walking with the wise; hang out
with fools and watch your life fall to pieces.

Proverbs 13:20 (Message)

Friends love through all kinds of weather, and families stick together in all kinds of trouble.

Proverbs 17:17 (Message)

If you've gotten anything at all out of following
Christ, if his love has made any difference in your
life, if being in a community of the Spirit means
anything to you, if you have a heart, if you care—
then do me a favor: Agree with each other, love each
other, be deep-spirited friends. Don't push your way
to the front; don't sweet-talk your way to the top.
Put yourself aside, and help others get ahead. Don't

be obsessed with getting your own advantage. Forget yourselves long enough to lend a helping hand.

Philippians 2:1-4 (Message)

It's better to have a partner than go it alone. Share the work, share the wealth. And if one falls down, the other helps, But if there's no one to help, tough!

Ecclesiastes 4:9-10 (Message)

Feeding Your Inner PK

A man who doesn't trust himself can never truly trust anyone else.

—Cardinal de Retz, Memoires

Do not trust all men, but trust men of worth; the former course is silly, the latter a mark of prudence.

—Democritus

You may be deceived if you trust too much, but you will live in torment if you do not trust enough.

—Frank Crane

We're never so vulnerable than when we trust someone—but paradoxically, if we cannot trust, neither can we find love or joy.

—Walter Anderson

The key is to get to know people and trust them to be who they are. Instead, we trust people to be who we want them to be—and when they're not, we cry.

—Anonymous

Additional Resources

Boundaries by Henry Cloud

Journal

Am I a person who is trusting of others? If not, why?

_____

_____

_____

_____

_____

_____

_____

_____

_____

_____

RICHARD M. SALAZAR JR.

What can I do right now to begin learning how to be trusting of others?

_____

_____

_____

_____

_____

_____

_____

_____

_____

Are there any relationships in my life that I don't trust? If so, why?

_____

_____

_____

_____

_____

_____

_____

_____

_____

What do I need to do in order to change these relationships?

_____

_____

_____

_____

_____

_____

_____

_____

_____

_____

My prayer asking God to show me how to be trusting of others and who to trust:

_____

_____

_____

_____

_____

_____

_____

_____

_____

Depression

If you look at the world, you'll be distressed. If you look within, you'll be depressed. If you look at God you'll be at rest.

—Corrie ten Boom

In his book *Fall to Grace: A Revolution of God, Grace and Society*, Jay Bakker gives readers a glimpse of what it was like to grow up as the son of the famously disgraced televangelists Jim and Tammy Faye Bakker. Before their fall, Bakker says his life was a fishbowl, but at least it was a nice fishbowl. After all, besides the largest Christian television network in the world, his parents ran a popular theme park, which Jay says he says he treated as his "own personal fiefdom."

Jay, like most preachers' kids, had to live with the fact that his own childhood was on public display. Of course, with a television audience of twelve million, the degree to which he had to grow up publically was exponentially multiplied. He recalls the humiliation, for example, of having his yearbook picture mailed to more than 600 thousand PTL followers around the world. Still, that kind of publicity can simply be an annoyance to be overcome unless your parents are catapulted into a descent driven by hidden sin that starts with drug addiction, includes an illicit affair, followed by a hush-money coverup, and ends with a father being carted off to prison. Bakker recalls:

> From the perspective of an eleven-year-old boy, the free fall was dizzying. One minute I was the scion of a famous family. The next I was a social leper with the most notorious last name in Christendom (besides Iscariot). I was so radioactive that my friends were literally forbidden to play with me. (Bakker and Edlund 2011)

Jim Bakker was sentenced to forty-five years in prison (he eventually served five). Young Jay watched it all, along with everyone else, on the news. "Dad was paraded, sobbing and shackled, through a gauntlet of TV cameras to the mental ward. It may have been great television, but it was torture for me to watch (Bakker and Edlund 2011)."

Jay Bakker's story is extreme, but the extremity is more about the vast public nature of his story versus the breakdown of his family. Not surprisingly, Jay descended into years of drug and alcohol abuse to drown out his pain and depression.

Every family suffers some degree of dysfunction. After all, families are made up of human beings, and human beings are flawed. Where a strong bond of love and grace are evident, though, the ebb and flow of family problems can be navigated. But when those crucial ingredients are absent, disaster eventually ensues.

Huge chasms between pulpit and home can be downright toxic to the children. As counselor Ruth Hetzendorfer writes, "Hypocrisy is murder to our kids. Watching a parent preach love, repentance, forgiveness, and holiness at church, then ripping his family apart because they don't measure up to certain expectations, breeds bitter feelings and eventually poisons the child (Hetzendorfer).

When the pastor and his family maintain false appearances publically, the stress of living a lie will evidence itself. Pastors' kids may suffer the most, because they often sacrifice their own chances for seeking help.

The stress of being forced into two lives—one public and one private—often leads to a feeling of powerlessness. And powerlessness can lead to depression. According to statistics compiled by Bill Bright from a number of resources, "Eighty percent of adult children of pastors surveyed have had to seek professional help for depression" (Blake, 2010).

Depression manifests itself in numerous ways, including but not limited to, feeling hopeless and helpless, an inability to control negative thinking no matter how much you try, an uncontrollable temper, and an overwhelming sense of worthlessness.

While it is not uncommon for most of us to experience some symptoms of depression from time to time, clinical depression occurs when those symptoms move in and set up permanent shop. In other words, they don't go away. It's as though you have climbed into a very deep, dark hole, and you cannot figure out how to get back out.

Besides the obvious need to seek professional support, it might help to consider how being raised as the son or daughter of a minister may have contributed to the depression. Identifying the contributing factors for your depression bring you that much closer to addressing them.

> **"**
>
> When you find yourself in
> that proverbial hole, remember
> that you are not powerless.
>
> **"**

My own struggle with depression stemmed from being surrounded at times by people who said they loved me but proved to be selfish Christians in their ambitions. So, for me, there were major implications. I dealt with anxiety. I had physical limitations to overcome, and I struggled with depression. To this day, I have to watch my propensity for depression carefully, and I have to continually rely on God's overcoming power in my life to win.

Many factors can contribute to depression, including genetics, biological issues, health issues, trauma, grief, medications, and more. But because pastors' kids so often know how to wear a public mask well, it may be harder for us to recognize depression or admit that it's a problem once we do see it.

Getting help means we have to remove that mask of bravado. When you find yourself in that proverbial hole, remember that you are not powerless. First and foremost, if you are a Christian, the Spirit of God lives within you. Scripture teaches that if God's Spirit has taken up shop within us, we do well to remember that the same Spirit raised Jesus from the dead.

> But if the Spirit of Him who raised Jesus from the dead dwells in you, He who raised Christ Jesus from the dead will also give life to your mortal bodies through His Spirit who dwells in you.
>
> Romans 8:11 (NASV)

That's an amazing power source right within you. So take heart. You are never alone. Besides going to God daily as your source for life and living, there are other practical steps you can take to deal with depression.

#1 Educate yourself.

There is a plethora of information available on depression and on both traditional and non-traditional treatments. Arm yourself with information so that you can ask the right questions of any professionals you seek out.

#2 Don't be afraid to seek help.

You might even start by confiding in a close friend. Don't be afraid, though, to seek professional help.

#3 Know that there's more than one option for treatment.

Because we are all unique, each of us responds differently to the same treatment. What works for one person may fail for the next. Don't be discouraged if it takes more than one attempt to find just the right combination for you.

#4 Get outside and get some exercise.

Good old-fashioned sunshine and endorphin-producing exercise, even in small amounts, can go a long, long way to helping you begin the climb back out of an emotional hole. Even getting away from your desk or place of work for a quick walk around the block can make a significant difference in your ability to zoom out and see things more clearly.

#5 Be purposeful about spending time with other people.

Depression often fuels itself on isolation. There is something about the healthy perspective you gain from being with other people that can help you deal with depression.

Just be sure to choose people who have some wisdom and grace and who understand your need for discretion.

Resource from the Source

You keep him in perfect peace whose mind is stayed on you, because he trusts in you.

Isaiah 26: 3

Do not fear, for I am with you; Do not anxiously look about you, for I am your God. I will strengthen you, surely I will help you, Surely I will uphold you with My righteous right hand.

Isaiah 41:10

Why are you down in the dumps, dear soul? Why are you crying the blues?
Fix my eyes on God—soon I'll be praising again. He puts a smile on my face. He's my God.

Psalm 42:5 (Message)

Submit therefore to God. Resist the devil and he will flee from you.

James 4:7 (NASB)

Feeding Your Inner PK

> A pearl is a beautiful thing that is produced by an injured life. It is the tear [that results] from the injury of the oyster. The treasure of our being in this world is also produced by an injured life. If we had not been wounded, if we had not been injured, then we will not produce the pearl.
>
> —Stephan Hoeller

> Character cannot be developed in ease and quiet. Only through experience of trial and suffering can the soul be strengthened, ambition inspired, and success achieved.
>
> —Helen Keller

> Pain insists upon being attended to. God whispers to us in our pleasures, speaks in our consciences, but shouts in our pains. It is his megaphone to rouse a deaf world.
>
> —C.S. Lewis

> What you thought before has led to every choice you have made, and this adds up to you at this moment. If you want to change who you are physically, mentally, and spiritually, you will have to change what you think.
>
> —Dr. Patrick Gentempo

Trials give you strength, sorrows give understanding and wisdom.

—Chuck T. Falcon

Additional Resources

www.afsp.org
www.webmd.com/depression/default.htm
www.newlife.com

Journal

What are some of the thoughts or circumstances causing me to be depressed?

_____

_____

_____

_____

_____

_____

_____

_____

_____

What steps have I taken to cope with my depression?

_____

_____

_____

_____

_____

_____

_____

_____

_____

_____

Which readily available Bible promises speak directly to my depression?

_____

_____

_____

_____

_____

_____

_____

_____

_____

I can speak with these three people right now to help me overcome my depression. List them:

_____

_____

_____

_____

_____

_____

_____

_____

_____

My prayer to God:

_____

_____

_____

_____

_____

_____

_____

_____

_____

What is God saying to me about my depression?

_____

_____

_____

_____

_____

_____

_____

_____

_____

Family

Sticking with your family is what makes it a family.

—Mitch Albom, *For One More Day*

The homes of pastors, many times, are not at all what they're cracked up to be. Most people think the homes PKs grow up in are pleasant, peaceful, holy, and in order. As they say in textville, lol!

When there are sons and daughters growing up in the home of pastors, there is sure to be chaos! This is just part of life. I mean, what home does not experience windstorms every now and then? Pastors' homes are *not* exempt from trials and tribulations by any means. We all live in a busy world, and we all have selfish needs and desires that keep our homes busy, and while busy, can become distracted and caught up in discord as a result. This is normal and will happen. How you respond, or what part you played in the eruption, is an opportunity for you to make things right again. Fault or no fault, the fact is you live in a home the enemy would love to ruin…plain and simple.

And here is a little secret that you probably already know…you are probably going to be the enemy's biggest target. I hate to drop that bomb on you, but it is true. If the enemy can't succeed at ruining your mom and dad, then you are his next best target. He knows that if he can get you to act out or betray your family, the next step is for there to be dissention and anger toward all members of the house. The result is a temporary broken home and a distraction from the ministry.

> If the enemy can't succeed at ruining your mom and dad, then you are his next best target.

As hard as it is, you must learn to find God's help for all family issues. He is the only one that can restore peace back into the home. Play your part, but don't overstep your boundaries. Mom and Dad are the leaders of the home, and they are required to lead the home back into happiness. As they do, you can take part by finding your place and making it happen. The key is to immediately identify the issues and find common ground where peace can once again reign in the home.

The following are six things you can do in your family to keep the environment healthy and productive. If you are a PK still living at home, you are not the leader of your home, so if your family is not doing any of these tips, why not respectfully suggest them today!

#1 Have family nights.

Whether it is a movie night or going out to a show, you as a family can find a deeper closeness by enjoying activities together.

#2 Family walks.

Get out into the neighborhood or a local park and get some family exercise in. This kind of activity creates a special interest for each other and brings the need for a healthy family back to the center of attention. Care for one another can grow deeper just by exercising together.

#3 Eat together.

This is one activity that often is missing in the home of pastors. Because Mom and Dad are so busy, they seldom bring the family together for dinner. This must be a daily discipline for every home of pastors, ministers, and missionaries. This is a time where various family issues can be discussed and remedied.

#4 Take vacations.

This has always been a tough one for the homes of pastors, ministers, and missionaries to be consistent in, but it must be more intentional so it will happen every year.

#5 Pray together.

Unfortunately, many pastors' homes do not spend time in prayer together. This has always baffled me. To think that pastors are neglecting something so spiritual in their home, yet they often wonder why their families are so broken. A pastor whose family prays together will stay together. This is not a new thought! Pastors are the spiritual leaders in the home and should be praying with their family every day.

Resource from the Source

By wisdom a house is built,
And by understanding it is established;
And by knowledge the rooms are filled
With all precious and pleasant riches.

Proverbs 24:3-4 (NASB)

The wicked are overthrown and are no more,
But the house of the righteous will stand.

Proverbs 12:7 (NASB)

Beyond all these things put on love, which is the perfect bond of unity. Let the peace of Christ rule in your hearts, to which indeed you were called in one body; and be thankful.

Colossians 3:14-15 (NASB)

For where two or three have gathered together in My name, I am there in their midst."

Matthew 18:20 (NASB)

Honor your father and mother so that you'll live a long time in the land that God, your God, is giving you.

Exodus 20:12 (Message)

Feeding Your Inner PK

Other things may change us, but we start and end with family.

—Anthony Brandt

The love of a family is life's greatest blessing.

—Anonymous

A happy family is but an earlier heaven.

—George Bernard

Family is the most important thing in the world.

—Princess Diana

Call it a clan, call it a network, call it a tribe, call it a family. Whatever you call it, whoever you are, you need one.

—Jane Howard

No matter where you live, brothers are brothers and sisters are sisters. The bonds that keep family close are the same no matter where you are.

—Anonymous

Journal

Do I regularly find a healthy commitment to happiness and unity in our home? If not, why not?

_____

_____

_____

_____

_____

_____

_____

_____

_____

_____

What are some of the creative things I can do to help improve our family relationships?

_____

_____

_____

_____

_____

_____

_____

_____

_____

Are we able to discuss our family issues honestly and openly? If not, what can I do to help create an open forum to share my thoughts?

_____

_____

_____

_____

_____

_____

_____

_____

_____

_____

How can I be more supportive of my parents spending more time with the ministry than with our family?

_____

_____

_____

_____

_____

_____

_____

_____

_____

_____

My prayer for our family:

_____

_____

_____

_____

_____

_____

_____

_____

_____

Mentors

Remember that mentor leadership is all about serving. Jesus said, "For even the Son of Man came not to be served but to serve others and to give his life as a ransom for many."

Mark 10:45
Tony Dungy,
The Mentor Leader: Secrets to Building People and
Teams That Win Consistently

The topic of trust is very similar to what will be discussed here. The reason is because it takes trust to have the kind of mentors you will need in your life in order to be successful in all you put your hands to. Without trusted mentors, it will almost be impossible to know exactly how to get to where it is you want to go in life. Mentors are designed to help guide you toward your dreams. Just like spiritual mentors are there to help you mature spiritually. Mentors are "must have" treasures in our life.

Without rehashing the trust chapter, let me remind you that without trust, you will never find the right mentors you need in your life. You must learn to trust people that God sends your way to help you achieve goals in life.

Let's define what a mentor is. The best definition of a mentor is this simple one: a mentor is someone who serves as a counselor or guide. Pretty easy to understand, yet pretty difficult to find. It is easy to define what a mentor is supposed to do for us, but it takes effort on your part to find that gem or two.

Most people underestimate the value of a mentor, and this is one of the biggest reasons for failure in business. A mentor offers valuable insight to things that only experience can teach, as well as a host of other things. They have fruit on their tree, which shows they have paid the price to be in a position to offer wisdom to you if you need it.

If you examine any successful person, they typically have one thing in common: a mentor. Nearly every successful person in history had someone who they could confide in and learn from when times were tough. To be successful in life it is very important to have a mentor, a coach, someone with more experience than you, someone who is in a position in life that you desire to be in the future.

When you look for a mentor, you need to look for someone who will come alongside you to motivate you, direct you, and encourage you in the way you should go.

Mentors are designed to help
guide you toward your dreams.

"

The following points will put into perspective the importance of having a good mentor and the peace of mind that comes with knowing you have someone in your corner who is knowledgeable about where you want to go in life. And believe me, if you don't have one yet, you better find one before you need one!

Use these five characteristics of a great mentor to help you when considering a potential mentor.

#1 Provides encouragement.

A mentor will encourage you when you are feeling low. The word *encouragement* means "to give courage," and a good mentor will provide just that. This does not mean that other people cannot offer you encouragement, but when those much-needed words come from someone who knows and understands your goals inside and out, it means a lot more. A good mentor will motivate you with a simple statement that affirms you are on the right track even when things do not seem to be going well. They have the ability to reassure you that everything is going as it should be, because they have been there before.

#2 Helps to reduce mistakes.

A mentor will help you prevent mistakes that you otherwise would have no way of avoiding. The Holy Spirit should be the tour guide of our lives. He is the final standard and the final source of wisdom in your life. However, there are basic life lessons that can help to guide you in your decision-making process.

Let me point out two practical ways to gain wisdom in life: first, making your own mistakes, and second, learning from others' mistakes. If you're thinking about walking through a minefield, you probably won't follow the path where there's an empty set of boots lying on the ground. A mentor has already made all the mistakes for you so you don't have to do it all over again. So in other words, experience is the best teacher *if* it's not your own experience. Failure is only possible if you decide to figure out everything on your own, because the problem with that route is that you don't have enough time to make all the mistakes you need to make to become successful.

#3 Helps to eliminate weaknesses.

A mentor will help you remove your weaknesses. This is usually the tougher aspect of a mentoring relationship, because it involves pruning off some of the things holding you back in life. If you have good mentors, you need to understand that you are not always going to like them. Their primary role is to be your mentor, and their secondary role is to be your friend. Your best friends see you as you are; your mentor sees you for who you can be. Your friends will tolerate your weaknesses, but your mentor will remove them entirely. Your friends are comfortable with your past, but your mentor is more comfortable with your future. A good mentor will stretch you just by being in your presence because they know and understand you better than you understand yourself.

#4 Helps to bring out your strengths.

The truth is that it takes a certain type of person to bring out talent and ability undeveloped in people. Talent cannot be taught, which is why coaches are more valuable than players. Without good coaches, talent would be useless. A good mentor will help bring out the best in you when you don't necessarily see the qualities you possess.

#5 Is honest.

A mentor will tell you the truth, because their primary objective is to make sure you are successful. Your friends will always tell you what you want to hear, but a mentor will tell you what you need to hear. This is not always easy to do because of ego issues, especially in men. But a good mentor understands that a day of tension is better than a lifetime of regret and as such will always tell you the truth rather than let you believe you have arrived at your destination.

Resource from the Source

Refuse good advice and watch your plans fail; take good counsel and watch them succeed.

Proverbs 15:22

One generation shall commend your works to another, and shall declare your mighty acts.

Psalm 145:4 (ESV)

So, my son, throw yourself into this work for Christ. Pass on what you heard from me—the whole congregation saying Amen!— to reliable leaders who are competent to teach others. When the going gets rough, take it on the chin with the rest of us, the way Jesus did. A soldier on duty doesn't get caught up in making deals at the marketplace. He concentrates on carrying out orders. An athlete who refuses to play by the rules will never get anywhere. It's the diligent farmer who gets the produce. Think it over. God will make it all plain.

2 Timothy 2:2 (Message)

Feeding Your Inner PK

There's a difference between interest and commitment. When you're interested in doing something, you do it only when it's convenient. When you're committed to something, you accept no excuses; only results.

—Kenneth Blanchard

The biggest difference is in the leadership. It was better for us. We had more coaches and mentors to help us. A lot of the younger players today suffer from a lack of direction.

—Isaiah Thomas

Be like a postage stamp. Stick to something until you get there.

—Josh Billings

Alexander the Great valued learning so highly, that he used to say he was more indebted to Aristotle for giving him knowledge than to his father Philip for life.

—Samuel Smiles

My chief want in life is someone who shall make me do what I can.

—Ralph Waldo Emerson

Mentoring is a brain to pick, an ear to listen, and a push in the right direction.

—John Crosby

Journal

Do I have at least one trusted mentor in my life? If not, why?

_____

_____

_____

_____

_____

_____

_____

_____

_____

Are any of these reasons valid compared to the spiritual and natural benefits of having a mentor?

What areas/issues in my life are in need of sound advice?

_____

_____

_____

_____

_____

_____

What would be some of the qualifiers for a trusted mentor in my life?

_____

_____

_____

_____

_____

_____

_____

_____

_____

_____

Who do I know that would qualify to be my mentor?

_____

_____

_____

_____

_____

_____

_____

_____

_____

What can I do right now to find the mentor I need in my life?

_____

_____

_____

_____

_____

_____

_____

_____

_____

The Mind

People are just as happy as they make up their minds to be.

—Abraham Lincoln

Each of us has access to an unlimited power. This power has a creative potential and energy that is hard to imagine. That power is the power contained in our thoughts. Our thoughts truly create our reality. If your thoughts are negative, it's pretty clear that you will live a negative life. If you think positive, you will live a positive, productive life, even when those tough times show up. Your thinking navigates where you go in life.

We have been created to live healthy, happy, successful lives. If our life is not like this, then we have helped to bring on the unhealthy, unhappy, unsuccessful conditions, which are denying us what is ours. And we have done so by our thoughts.

You, and you alone, are responsible for your thoughts. Nobody in the world can put a thought in your head without your permission. Your mind belongs to you! It's your job to control your thoughts! You are the master of your mind, and you are the guardian of your thoughts. Only you can determine what they will be, and only you can change them.

> "
> You are the master of your mind, and you are the guardian of your thoughts. Only you can determine what they will be, and only you can change them.
> "

Your mind is incredible. The brain has been compared to a computer in a sort of bio-computer analogy. Science has discovered many of the hard-wired connections that appear to give the brain/mind so much control over the body (health, wellness, longevity, youthfulness) and our destinies in terms of success, learning, wealth, and prosperity.

God wants us to be smart. He wants us to use our brains and consider what we do, to make good decisions using logic—not our emotions. To become an expert in thinking wholesome, fruitful thoughts takes practice, practice, practice. It's just like disciplining ourselves to learn a dance routine, a musical instrument, or a program on the computer. To become adept at thinking godly thoughts takes noticing your thought processes and comparing them to the truth, God's Word.

As PKs we are constantly bombarded with thoughts—thoughts that are so overwhelming it can drive us to spend most of our time thinking negatively about our lives. God wants to show you so much, and the only way for us to process and comprehend those revelations is with a healthy mind. When you find yourself thinking and rethinking thoughts that distract you from what's true, stop! Cast them over to your heavenly Father. Replace those thoughts with the "excellent and praiseworthy." This takes some real conscious effort, but the end result is peace. When you give your distractions to God, you will experience the peace He has promised. It is peace that stands guard over your heart and mind, peace that allows for good fruit to flourish in your life.

Here are five steps to take control of your thought life:

#1 Control your mind confidently.

Your mind is the greatest miracle in the universe. Everyone has an amazing treasure——a brain and nerves. Every normal person basically has the power to reach everything that others can or try to reach. You have the power to aim the spirit, emotion, instinct, willingness, feelings, mood, attitude, and act to obtain a result.

#2 Focus your mind to what you really want and get rid of what you don't want.

Most of your mind patterns will be replaced by words, but the deepest motivational thinking uses pictures, not words. If an idea appears, it is usually as a picture, not a moving sentence of words in our head. Pictures are the earliest and strongest mind pattern. So we have to learn to discipline our mind and visualize things that we want. Don't let environment or other people dictate negative images into your mind.

#3 Get rid of all negative thoughts through self inspection.

Most people do not realize that they are having negative thoughts unless they are consciously trying to inspect their own mind. Just ask yourself, "Is this positive or negative?" When we fail to conquer our mind, our reaction will tend to be negative. The more we train to use positive mental attitude, the faster we realize the decrease in negative thoughts.

#4 Read God's Word.

The way to think godly thoughts is to purpose to spend time in the Word of God every day and to renew your mind with it. You have to get God's Word into your spirit so that your soul (your mind) becomes renewed to God's will. God's Word is His will. When you have godly thoughts, they lead to godly thoughts and actions.

#5 Use the power of prayer.

When you pray, believe in anything you ask. God will give you the added power you need to overcome negative thinking!

Resource from the Source

This book of the law shall not depart from your mouth, but you shall meditate on it day and night, so that you may be careful to do according to all that is written in it; for then you will make your way prosperous, and then you will have success.

Joshua 1:8 (NASB)

Trust in the LORD with all your heart
And do not lean on your own understanding.

Proverbs 3:5 (NASB)

So here's what I want you to do, God helping you: Take your everyday, ordinary life—your sleeping, eating, going-to-work, and walking-around life— and place it before God as an offering. Embracing what God does for you is the best thing you can do for him. Don't become so well-adjusted to your culture that you fit into it without even thinking. Instead, fix your attention on God. You'll be changed from the inside out. Readily recognize what he wants from you, and quickly respond to it. Unlike the culture around you, always dragging you down to its level of immaturity, God brings the best out of you, develops well-formed maturity in you.

Romans 12:2 (Message)

Summing it all up, friends, I'd say you'll do best by filling your minds and meditating on things true, noble, reputable, authentic, compelling, gracious—the best, not the worst; the beautiful, not the ugly; things to praise, not things to curse. Put into practice what you learned from me, what you heard and saw and realized. Do that, and God, who makes everything work together, will work you into his most excellent harmonies.

Philippians 4:8 (Message)

Feeding Your Inner PK

Watch your thoughts, for they become words.
Watch your words, for they become actions.
Watch your actions, for they become habits.
Watch your habits, for they become character.
Watch your character, for it becomes your destiny.

—Anonymous

As you begin changing your thinking, start immediately to change your behavior. Begin to act the part of the person you would like to become. Take action on your behavior. Too many people want to feel, then take action. This never works.

—John Maxwell

A man is but the product of his thoughts, what he thinks, he becomes.

—Anonymous

Positive anything is better than negative nothing.

—Elbert Hubbard

The positive thinker sees the invisible, feels the intangible, and achieves the impossible.

—Anonymous

Once you replace negative thoughts with positive ones, you'll start having positive results.

—Willie Nelson

Journal

What thoughts do I struggle with daily?

_____

_____

_____

_____

_____

_____

_____

_____

_____

Which of these thoughts regularly interfere with my relationship with God?

_____

_____

_____

_____

_____

_____

_____

_____

_____

What outward stimuli trigger my bad thinking?

_____

_____

_____

What promises in God's Word can apply to my thoughts?

_____

_____

_____

My prayer to God asking for added power to start changing the way I think:

_____

_____

_____

_____

_____

_____

_____

_____

_____

Hurts

The LORD is a stronghold for the oppressed, a stronghold in times of trouble.

Psalms 9:9

Most people react to hurt by trying to do something about it. Physical injury often requires some sort of physical treatment. Physical injury can also be treated, in part, with mental imagery and prayer. A wound, for example, has to be cleaned and bandaged and cared for with positive thoughts of its healing. Emotional pain, however, presents more of a problem. Many people treat emotional pain by hiding it; that is, they do something self-gratifying—such as drink alcohol, use drugs, have sex, gamble, watch TV or movies, eat sweets or fats, and so on—that numbs the pain but that does nothing to heal it.

Many people also use anger and revenge to respond to hurt.

Without a doubt, all PKs will experience hurt from time to time, whether that hurt comes from people in the church, our friends, and even from family. Hurt is an inevitable part of our life. So it's not a matter of if you will get hurt, it is only a matter of when. And you should be prepared if you're going to survive. I wish there was a way to make that pain go away fast and easy, but depending on how badly you were violated, some hurts tend to stick around for a while.

Being emotionally hurt and not being able to get past it has happened to all of us at some point in our lives, and as I've often said, "It's not easy getting past the emotional pain someone has caused you." Of course if you're only dealing with the pain from one situation that caused you to be emotionally hurt, then I would consider you one of the blessed ones. The only way I'm able to deal with hurt is to decide what I want in my life—pain or joy, sadness or happiness, lack or abundance.

> **Without a doubt, all PKs will experience hurt from time to time, whether that hurt comes from people in the church, our friends, and even from family.**

And you must decide. These emotional hurts are locked away, but their radioactivity is leaking out. In order to get rid of the radioactivity contained in the box, you first have to trace the box. In order to trace the box, I would suggest that you pray that the Holy Spirit reveal it to you. The Holy Spirit will then start to bring to mind all the hurts that have been sealed away but never properly dealt with. Disinfect the hurts with forgiveness, clean them with the blood of Jesus, and cover them with the plaster of love, and soon the hurts will heal totally with no further radioactivity, for they are cleansed, disinfected, covered properly, and healed forever. Sound too easy? Well, it's not! It does take hard work to release those hurts back to God. But if you don't, you will run into all sorts of spiritual setbacks, not to mention the many physical ones as well.

Underlying much of our behavior is what is called a belief system. This system within us filters what we see and hear, affecting how we behave in our daily lives. There are many other elements that affect our lives, including our past and core issues that we're born with, but our belief systems in this life have a major effect on what we think and do.

It takes a lot of work to look at yourself and identify the beliefs that are affecting your life in a negative manner. However, knowing your beliefs will give you a sound basis for emotional freedom. I do believe that it's wise to deal with the belief systems before dealing with the identification and release of emotions.

Resource from the Source

He heals the brokenhearted
And binds up their wounds.

Psalm 147:3 (NASB)

Many are the afflictions of the righteous,
But the LORD delivers him out of them all.

Psalm 34:19 (NASB)

If your heart is broken, you'll find God right there;
if you're kicked in the gut, he'll help you catch your
breath.

Psalm 34:18 (Message)

In prayer there is a connection between what God
does and what you do. You can't get forgiveness
from God, for instance, without also forgiving others. If you refuse to do your part, you cut yourself off
from God's part.

Matthew 6:14-15 (Message)

Make a clean break with all cutting, backbiting,
profane talk. Be gentle with one another, sensitive.
Forgive one another as quickly and thoroughly as
God in Christ forgave you.

Ephesians 4:32 (Message)

Feeding Your Inner PK

Love comes to those who still hope even though
they've been disappointed, to those who still believe
even though they've been betrayed, to those who
still love even though they've been hurt before.

—Neil Gaiman

I've learned that no matter how good a friend someone is, they're going to hurt you every once in awhile and you must forgive them for that.

—Neil Gaiman

Nobody can hurt me without my permission.

—Mohandas Gandhi

But pain insists upon being attended to. God whispers to us in our pleasures, speaks in our conscience, but shouts in our pains: it is His megaphone to rouse a deaf world.

—C.S. Lewis

Life is 10 percent what happens to you, and 90 percent how you respond to it.

—Unknown

Journal

What hurts am I carrying in my heart? Why?

_____

_____

_____

_____

_____

_____

_____

_____

_____

How are these hurts keeping me from living free and happy?

_____

_____

_____

_____

_____

_____

_____

_____

_____

_____

Are any of these hurts an overreaction? If so, what can I do right now to release them to God?

_____

_____

_____

_____

_____

_____

_____

_____

_____

_____

What steps can I take right now to forgive those who have hurt me?

_____

_____

_____

_____

_____

_____

_____

_____

_____

_____

What promises are found in God's Word that can bring healing to my heart?

_____

_____

_____

_____

_____

_____

_____

_____

_____

My prayer to God asking Him to give me the inner strength to release all hurts to Him:

_____

_____

_____

_____

_____

_____

_____

_____

_____

_____

Rejection

A rejection is nothing more than a necessary step in the pursuit of success.

—Bo Bennett

The topic of rejection is probably the most difficult one for me to write about because of the rejection I experienced growing up as a PK. However, there are many PKs out there who never experience rejection, or for that matter, any of the issues in this book. But for most PKs, rejection is something that they have had to deal with most of their lives, and even become so marginalized that they live their adult lives secluded. They have families and live regular lives, but they do all this in the shadows of life.

Rejection is simply the result of living with the fear that others will not accept you for who you are, what you believe, and how you act. Now, there can be many reasons why you might be feeling rejected. Whether it's because of your position, or maybe you just need to brush up on your social skills. Whatever the reason, the fact is rejection can hurt deeply. We have all been rejected at one time or another, and we have all felt the pain associated with

RICHARD M. SALAZAR JR.

the rebuff. The feelings of social rejection hurt in the same manner as that of physical pain.

When you find yourself in the role of a PK, it is rare that someone will prep you for what's to come. It is rare that someone will sit you down, look you straight in the eye, and say, "Little Buffy, you are now in the role of a PK the rest of your life, and this means you will be rejected by a lot of people, including friends quite often." I mean, who has the guts to say that to us! Again, the reason for this book is to help you understand what you will face in life, and rejection is a big one.

As a PK, just as all human beings, we have a strong need to feel secure. When you feel your sense of security is threatened; you may feel abandoned, scared, and/or hopeless. Under the circumstances it is understandable that you feel insecure. You may be wondering when the next blow will come and from which direction. It is important that you don't start to worry about that and that you immediately give that worry over to God. Before long, that sense of impending doom will eventually disappear.

Why are you afraid of getting rejected? Is it because you have to seem like you're perfect because you're the pastor's kid? Have you been taught to keep up a charade and not allow others to see your weaknesses? For a long time I battled with perfectionism, and it led me to reject rejection. I was in my own imaginary world and refused to face reality. It wasn't until I started letting go of trying to be perfect that I started making fast progress. It's okay to show people that you aren't Zeus, the Greek god! We all have vulnerabilities, and we all make mistakes. If you show some of them to the people you hang out with, they will just be able to relate to you more.

"

> Remember, a lot of rejection is not the actual rejection but how you handle it.

"

What would happen if you were never rejected? Would you grow as a human being? Would you need to grow? If everyone says yes to you, you wouldn't need to change anything, and you wouldn't need to learn anything. That would be a pretty boring life, wouldn't it? Learning how to deal with rejection is tough. Depending on how you get rejected and what for, it may hurt a lot, or it may hurt a little. Getting rejected is one of the best learning opportunities, that is, if you pay attention and learn from the experience. If you get rejected and blame someone else, you're probably not going to get much out of the interaction. If, however, you start thinking about what you could've done better, you're on to something. If you can't figure it out, ask the person who rejected you.

Here are six ways to effectively handle rejection:

#1 Don't take it personally.

There will always be a reason for rejection, whether it's because you were turned down for a job or you were too late getting in on an event with friends or just simply because you are the son or daughter of a pastor. The list will be endless on this one. Some rejections have nothing to do with us. So if you got turned down, do not second-guess that you are no good or that no one likes you. It may just be a question of timing!

#2 Listen to the rejection carefully.

It is important to pay attention to the reason for the rejection. This will tell you if you have a second chance or not. I would love to tell you that all rejection is not your fault, but the fact remains that at times we are responsible for our own rejection. So study the reasons for experiencing rejection and allow God to work it out in your favor either way!

#3 Have confidence in who you are.

Learn to have confidence that people will like you just as you are and to make yourself the best you that you can be for others. Learn how to educate yourself in what's going on around you, find out what others like to do or talk about, and learn what is happening in your world in order stay relevant.

#4 Know that everyone gets rejected.

There are six billion people on this earth. Knowing that rejection is an emotion that everybody experiences is a reality check! Don't allow a victim mentality to overtake you. Know that you are not alone and that God is on your side!

#5 Be kind to yourself.

Being rejected is a disappointment to say the least. It can be very frustrating to put yourself out there for either personal or professional reasons and then be told no. So be kind to yourself after getting rejected in some way. Engage in positive self-talk and encourage yourself for the future.

#6 Try and try again.

Do not, therefore, take rejection as a sign of failure. Instead, press on in your dreams!

Remember, a lot of rejection is not the actual rejection but how you handle it. If you engage in positive self-talk and have a confident attitude, it is possible to attract a better outcome.

Resource from the Source

Ready to rescue you.
If your heart is broken, you'll find GOD right there;

if you're kicked in the gut, he'll help you catch your
    breath.
Disciples so often get into trouble;
still, GOD is there every time.

Psalm 34:17-19 (Message)

And coming to Him as to a living stone which has
been rejected by men, but is choice and precious in
the sight of God,

1 Peter 2:4

And He has said to me, "My grace is sufficient
for you, for power is perfected in weakness." Most
gladly, therefore, I will rather boast about my weaknesses, so that the power of Christ may dwell in me.

2 Corinthians 12:9

Feeding Your Inner PK

A rejection is nothing more than a necessary step in
the pursuit of success.

—Bo Bennett

I take rejection as someone blowing a bugle in my
ear to wake me up and get going, rather than retreat.

—Sylvester Stallone

There's nothing like rejection to make you do an inventory of yourself.

—James Lee Burke

We keep going back, stronger, not weaker, because we will not allow rejection to beat us down. It will only strengthen our resolve. To be successful there is no other way.

—Graves, Earl G.

Journal

Why am I feeling rejected?

_____

_____

_____

_____

_____

_____

_____

_____

_____

Which of my actions are causing me to be rejected? Why?

_____

_____

_____

_____

_____

_____

_____

_____

_____

Is there something I am doing to be rejected by others? If so, what?

_____

_____

_____

_____

_____

_____

_____

_____

_____

_____

List the specific people that are shunning you. Why are they shunning you?

_____

_____

_____

_____

_____

_____

_____

_____

_____

_____

Are any of these reasons legitimate?

_____

_____

_____

_____

_____

_____

_____

_____

_____

Is there something I can do to be more of a team player?

_____

_____

_____

_____

_____

_____

_____

_____

What does God's Word say to help me handle rejection?

_____

_____

_____

_____

_____

_____

_____

_____

_____

_____

Discouragement

> The Christian life is not a constant high. I have my moments of deep discouragement. I have to go to God in prayer with tears in my eyes, and say, "O God, forgive me," or "Help me."
>
> —Billy Graham

Are you tired of being discouraged? You don't have to stay that way. Whether or not the situation changes, you can experience joy, peace, and contentment. For the believer, circumstances don't have to dictate emotions.

Everyone will have their share of discouragement at some point in their lifetime. However, our approach to managing our discouragement will distinguish us from others.

The dictionary defines discouragement as follows: "a feeling of despair in the face of obstacles; or a state of distraught and loss of sense of enthusiasm, drive or courage" (The Free Dictionary 2003-2012).

We can choose to remain discouraged or determine to work through our feelings and overcome them.

Discouragement happens in all areas of life. The root word of discouragement is courage, so it should only make sense that the feelings associated with failure and rejection often try to deal a blow to your inner source of courage. Unfortunately, these emotions can cripple you to the point where you avoid taking small risks that have huge potential rewards.

Getting discouraged is easy. There are negative people all around us, and it's hard to pick out which ones are being constructive and honest versus those who are being heavy handed. What you will find interesting is just how easy it is to let their opinion scuttle your mood for a while. That surely is a lot of power you're giving them. It's easy to get discouraged.

When our expectations aren't met, we feel disappointed. But discouragement, a feeling of despair and despondency, is a choice. We can choose to remain discouraged or determine to work through our feelings and overcome them.

There are three levels of discouragement. The first level is mild discouragement, when only our emotions are affected. The second level is stronger discouragement, when your spirit is affected. At this point, other people begin to notice something is wrong, that you are not yourself. Your friends, family, spouse, classmates, co-workers or the people at your church see that something is wrong. Your spirit is noticeably affected. The third level is disabling discouragement, the worst kind. This discouragement renders it impossible for the discouraged person to handle the normal responsibilities of life.

Here are four actions you can take right now to break the cycle of discouragement:

#1 Do something creative.

If you're recovering from a particularly disappointing setback, getting new ideas won't be easy. Look deep down inside of you and draw out what God is asking you to do… and go for it!

#2 Spend time with someone who isn't discouraged.

Time in that person's positive presence will naturally make you feel better yourself.

#3 Reorganize your life.

In other words, evaluate your use of time, energy, and other resources. Make sure you're doing the right things in the right way.

#4 Get guidance from a Christian counselor.

If your discouragement has become so deep that you're struggling to overcome it, share your concerns with a Christian counselor who can give you biblical advice about how to move forward.

Resource from the Source

No man will be able to stand before you all the days of your life. Just as I have been with Moses, I will be with you; I will not fail you or forsake you. Be strong and courageous, for you shall give this people possession of the land, which I swore to their fathers to give them.

Joshua 1:5-6 (NASB)

Why are you down in the dumps, dear soul?
Why are you crying the blues?
Fix my eyes on God—
soon I'll be praising again.
He puts a smile on my face.
He's my God.

Psalm 42:11 (Message)

From my distress I called upon the LORD;
The LORD answered me and set me in a large place.

Psalm 118:5 (NASB)

Casting all your anxiety on Him, because He cares for you.

1 Peter 5:7 (NASB)

Feeding Your Inner PK

Develop success from failures. Discouragement and failure are two of the surest stepping stones to success.

—Dale Carnegie

The Christian life is not a constant high. I have my moments of deep discouragement. I have to go to God in prayer with tears in my eyes, and say, "O God, forgive me," or "Help me."

—Billy Graham

The most essential factor is persistence—the determination never to allow your energy or enthusiasm to be dampened by the discouragement that must inevitably come.

—James Whitcomb Riley

Disappointments will come and go, but discouragement is a choice that you make.

—Dr. Charles Stanley

Let no feeling of discouragement prey upon you, and in the end you are sure to succeed.

—Abraham Lincoln

Journal

Who or what is causing me to feel discouraged?

_____

_____

_____

_____

_____

_____

_____

_____

_____

_____

What can I do right now to change how I feel?

_____

_____

_____

_____

_____

_____

_____

_____

_____

What are God's promises for my life when I am feeling discouraged?

_____

_____

_____

_____

_____

_____

_____

_____

_____

_____

Who can I talk with to help bring joy to my life when I am feeling discouraged?

_____

_____

_____

_____

_____

_____

_____

_____

_____

My prayer asking God for a courageous spirit:

_____

_____

_____

_____

_____

_____

_____

_____

_____

Forgiveness

Forgiveness must be immediate, whether or not a person asks for it. Trust must be rebuilt over time. Trust requires a track record.

—Rick Warren, *The Purpose Driven Life: What on Earth Am I Here For?*

We all have things that happen to us in life that create pain, anger, and grief. In most cases they come unexpectedly and are rarely deserved.

Forgiveness does not come easy for most of us. Our natural instinct is to recoil in self-protection when we've been injured. We don't naturally overflow with mercy, grace, and forgiveness when we've been wronged. Every Christian knows that Jesus instructed us that forgiveness should have no limits. Forgiveness is a continuing process. You just don't forgive and move on. That sore spot will continue to show up again and again. And in such situations, we must remember to forgive again and again.

C.S. Lewis put it this way: "We find that the work of forgiveness has to be done over and over again. We forgive, we mortify our resentment; a week later some chain of thought carries us back to the original offense and we discover the old resentment blazing away if nothing had been done about it at all. We need to forgive our brother seventy times seven not only for 490 offenses but for one offense."

Forgiveness is not only a struggle, but it's a very important struggle. If we truly want to live in communion with God, then we have to learn to forgive as He forgave. The real lesson to be learned is that the struggle to forgive is the struggle to be like Jesus.

> **"**
> Forgiveness is not granted because a person deserves to be forgiven.
> It is an act of love, mercy, and grace. **"**

The word *forgive* means to wipe the slate clean, to pardon, to cancel a debt. When we wrong someone, we seek his or her forgiveness in order for the relationship to be restored. It is important to remember that forgiveness is not granted because a person deserves to be forgiven. Instead, it is an act of love, mercy, and grace. How we act toward that person may change. It doesn't mean we will put ourselves back into a harmful situation or that we suddenly accept or approve of the person's continued wrong behavior. It simply means we release them from the wrong they committed against us. We forgive them because God forgave us.

Forgiveness. It's such a hard thing to do, but it can be so liberating to the soul. What makes it difficult for most of us to do is the way we define it. We think of forgiveness as meaning that we should say all is forgotten and things will go back to what they were. This biblical definition of forgiveness is very hard for most of us to swallow. How can you forget the unforgettable? How can you forgive the unforgivable? To enjoy the benefits of forgiveness, however, we needn't go that far. All that's really required is that we make the decision to move forward, to let go of the old hurts. We don't have to condone what's been done. What's wrong is still wrong. We don't have to invite the person back into our lives or even be friendly with them. What we do have to do is allow ourselves to release all the negative emotions associated with that person. As long as we hold onto the pain, we are choosing to allow that person's past actions to continue to hurt us. We can also choose to stop letting them hurt us. That's a definition of forgiveness that's more doable for those who are less than saintly!

There are times we don't feel like forgiving those who have wronged us. It is easier to act our way into feeling than to feel our way into acting. Having a nature of not forgiving others brings about bitterness, and bitterness has been linked to stress-related illnesses by some medical researchers. By forgiving others we free ourselves spiritually and emotionally. Forgiveness is an act of our own personal will in obedience and submission to God's will, trusting God to bring emotional healing.

Resource from the Source

Overlook an offense and bond a friendship; fasten on to a slight and—good-bye, friend!

Proverbs 17:9 (Message)

In prayer there is a connection between what God does and what you do. You can't get forgiveness from God, for instance, without also forgiving others. If you refuse to do your part, you cut yourself off from God's part.

Matthew 6:14 (Message)

At that point Peter got up the nerve to ask, "Master, how many times do I forgive a brother or sister who hurts me? Seven?" Jesus replied, "Seven! Hardly. Try seventy times seven."

Matthew 18:21-22

My heavenly Father will also do the same to you, if each of you does not forgive his brother from your heart.

Matthew 18:35 (NASB)

I encourage you to read the entire story in Matthew 18:21-35.

So, chosen by God for this new life of love, dress in the wardrobe God picked out for you: compassion, kindness, humility, quiet strength, discipline. Be even-tempered, content with second place, quick to forgive an offense. Forgive as quickly and completely as the Master forgave you. And regardless of what else you put on, wear love. It's your basic, all-purpose garment. Never be without it.

Colossians 3:13 (Message)

Feeding Your Inner PK

When you hold resentment toward another, you are bound to that person or condition by an emotional link that is stronger than steel. Forgiveness is the only way to dissolve that link and get free.

—Catherine Ponder

To forgive is the highest, most beautiful form of love. In return, you will receive untold peace and happiness.

—Robert Muller

When a deep injury is done us, we never recover until we forgive.

—Alan Paton

Forgiveness is not an occasional act. It is a permanent attitude.

—Martin Luther King Jr.

Anger makes you smaller, while forgiveness forces you to grow beyond what you were.

—Cherie Carter-Scott

I firmly believe a great many prayers are not answered because we are not willing to forgive someone.

—D.L. Moody

Journal

Am I generally a forgiving person? If not, why?

_____

_____

_____

_____

_____

_____

_____

_____

_____

This is a list of all those I am currently holding a grudge against:

_____

_____

_____

_____

_____

_____

_____

_____

_____

What steps can I take right now to forgive others?

_____

_____

_____

_____

_____

_____

_____

_____

_____

_____

This is a list of all those of whom I need to ask forgiveness:

_____

_____

_____

_____

_____

_____

_____

_____

_____

_____

What can I do right now to begin the forgiving process?

_____

_____

_____

_____

_____

_____

_____

_____

_____

What does God's Word tell me about forgiving others?

_____

_____

_____

_____

_____

_____

_____

_____

_____

My prayer to God asking for courage to forgive those who have hurt me:

_____

_____

_____

_____

_____

_____

_____

_____

_____

_____

The Church

You can be committed to Church but not committed to Christ, but you cannot be committed to Christ and not committed to church.

—Joel Osteen

Here is how I would define the church from the view of most PKs: the church is like another room in a home that we live in. The sanctuary is like a giant living room with the largest surround sound system ever known.

In other words, we don't always see the church as a holy place. For most PKs, the church is just another hangout place, a place where God is but where hundreds of people gather for us to hang out with. If you were raised in the church, it is common for you to feel a different kind of experience from those who were not. People who come into the church and are born again tend to have more of a reverence and respect for the physical structure we call the church. It is common for PKs to easily lose interest in the activities of the church, or it becomes the norm and routine so much so that we just don't believe in the point behind many of the activities of the church.

> **"**
> God wants us to work together
> so that the church body can minister to
> others more effectively.
> **"**

I remember growing up in the church and into my young adult years looking at all of the various ministries and thinking, *What's the point?* Why do we have these ministries? I even got to the point of looking out at the masses of people coming to our church and think, *Why are you all here?*

I became calloused to God's work even right down to the salvation of the sinner. It wouldn't move me. I would feel numb at the very fact that people on their way to hell were now headed for heaven. This is a very ugly place to be. Unfortunately, there are thousands of PKs all over the world who are in this same spot. Is it wrong to feel this way? No! You are human, and human nature, the fleshly side of us, no matter how important the environment, can deceive us into becoming cold to the things of God. It is not wrong to feel this way just as long as you catch yourself and ask God to give you a heart of compassion for His house once again.

I don't need to remind you of how important the church is and why you should work to keep its importance relevant in your life. In a broad biblical sense, the church is the body of Christ—the collection of Christian believers from all over the world and from all times who are bound together by the shed blood of Christ and His resurrected presence. In our local congregations we play an important part of the body of Christ. God wants us to work together so that the church body can minister to others more effectively.

My suggestion would be to get more involved in a ministry within the church. If you find yourself at a place where everything, every activity, every ministry in the church begins to become irrelevant in your life, find a ministry that is closest to reaching the unbeliever and commit yourself to it until you begin falling in love with the work of the Lord being done through the local church!

Here is another idea…become a member! Most PKs that I talk to have never become members of their own church. They just assume that they are because Mom and Dad are the pastors. Not true! Go through the membership classes. By doing this you will gain a new perspective on the church, and at the same time it will help you to see better what others experience and feel.

Here are four reasons why the local church should be taken seriously:

1. God is not merely concerned about our own private piety, but also about our care for the other sheep.
2. God wants us to encourage weaker Christians and run the race with them.
3. God wants us to see ourselves as providers, coming to serve others and not just to be served.

4. Your membership in a local church is important because it is there that you can hear the sound preaching and teaching of God's Word within the context of corporate worship.

Resource from the Source

And He gave some as apostles, and some as prophets, and some as evangelists, and some as pastors and teachers, for the equipping of the saints for the work of service, to the building up of the body of Christ; until we all attain to the unity of the faith, and of the knowledge of the Son of God, to a mature man, to the measure of the stature which belongs to the fullness of Christ.

Ephesians 4:11-13 (NASB)

Jesus, undeterred, went right ahead and gave his charge: "God authorized and commanded me to commission you: Go out and train everyone you meet, far and near, in this way of life, marking them by baptism in the threefold name: Father, Son, and Holy Spirit. Then instruct them in the practice of all I have commanded you. I'll be with you as you do this, day after day after day, right up to the end of the age."

Matthew 28:18-20 (Message)

O Lord, I love the habitation of Your house
And the place where Your glory dwells.

Psalm 26:8 (NASB)

I'm asking God for one thing, only one thing:
To live with him in his house my whole life long.
I'll contemplate his beauty; I'll study at his feet.

Psalm 27:4 (Message)

Those who are planted in the house of the Lord
shall flourish in the courts of our God.

Psalm 92:13 (NKJV)

The whole congregation of believers was united as one—one heart, one mind! They didn't even claim ownership of their own possessions. No one said, "That's mine; you can't have it." They shared everything. The apostles gave powerful witness to the resurrection of the Master Jesus, and grace was on all of them.

And so it turned out that not a person among them was needy. Those who owned fields or houses sold them and brought the price of the sale to the apostles and made an offering of it. The apostles then distributed it according to each person's need.

Acts 4:32-35 (Message)

Feeding Your Inner PK

Anyone who is to find Christ must first find the church. How could anyone know where Christ is and what faith is in him unless he knew where his believers are?

—Martin Luther

Church attendance is as vital to a disciple as a transfusion of rich, healthy blood to a sick man.

—Dwight L. Moody

For millions of men and women, the church has been the hospital for the soul, the school for the mind and the safe depository for moral ideas.

—Gerald R. Ford

Christianity means a lot more than church membership.

—Billy Sunday

Going to church doesn't make you a Christian any more than going to a garage makes you an automobile.

—Billy Sunday

Journal

How important is the church I attend to me?

_____

_____

_____

_____

_____

_____

_____

_____

_____

_____

Have I become too familiar with God's house that it has no real meaning to me anymore? If so, why?

_____

_____

_____

_____

_____

_____

_____

_____

_____

What does God's Word teach me about the importance of His house?

_____

_____

_____

_____

_____

_____

_____

_____

_____

_____

What steps can I take to develop a deeper reverence for God's house?

_____

_____

_____

_____

_____

_____

RICHARD M. SALAZAR JR.

_____

_____

_____

_____

Location

The real winners in life are the people who look at every situation with the expectation that they can make it work or make it better.

—Barbara Pletcher

This chapter is kind of the fluke chapter. It is a chapter that gives me the most excitement to write, because it has to do with living life not knowing where you will be living the day after tomorrow! If you are living in a place that you did not grow up in, or have moved from town to town or country to country, this chapter is for you. Like many others, I grew up with parents who were called to lead church plants around the country and abroad. One day we were living in one town, and the next day we were packing to move overseas. This is kind of how my life was during my growing-up years. We just never knew where we were going to be living next.

This kind of lifestyle can be hard on all aspects of life, especially if one day you are living in the United States of America, and the next month you're living in a foreign country. This can mess with your emotions, the way you think, and a host of other issues that you face as a traveling PK. Moving can be very difficult for some, especially if you are a teenager and you are not used to it; however, there comes a time when you have to face the facts and handle moving.

> **"** Since you are a part of God's call on Mom and Dad, find out what part you play in the ministry and get involved. **"**

As you prepare to move, if you are, you may feel as if you are planning two simultaneous moves: relocating to your new home and moving out of your current location. You could feel pulled in different directions, as the stress of your pending move continues to rise.

The emotional symptoms of relocation stress are varied. Some people feel irritable or impatient. Others may become moody, depressed, or withdrawn. They may have nightmares, cry frequently, or experience feelings of panic.

Here are five tips to help you make the transition easier:

#1 Immediately connect with new friends.

The one thing I needed the day we arrived in our new home in Farnworth, England, was friends…and I needed them badly! So try to connect with others in your neighborhood, and begin developing good relationships.

#2 Find out what social activities are available in your area.

You need to have social activities in your life. Find out everything there is to do for fun in your town. Once you know what to do and where these places are, go have fun!

#3 Find your place.

Since you are a part of God's call on Mom and Dad, find out what part you play in the ministry and get involved. Enjoy the ministry. There is no better thrill than to see God use us when we allow Him to. Get out there and let God do some amazing things through you, no matter your age. Find some people you can connect with, and share God with them. You will be amazed at the results!

#4 Discover your purpose.

As you begin to share God with others, you will start uncovering your lifelong purpose. Once you begin to know, the next best thing you can do for yourself is to begin writing down everything God shows you about your future. From this, you can start mapping out your future, and as a result, you will be so immersed in wanting to pursue your future, that it won't matter that you are in another town, state, or country.

#5 Stay focused on God.

Keep God number one in your life. In all that you put your hands to, make sure God is kept at the center of attention in your life. The only way to survive the life as a PK moving around the world is to work at strengthening your relationship with God. He is the only one who can keep you in perfect peace!

Resource from the Source

> Do not let your heart be troubled; believe in God, believe also in Me.
>
> John 14:1 (NASB)

> Casting all your anxiety on Him, because He cares for you.
>
> 1 Peter 5:7 (NASB)

> I will lift up my eyes to the mountains;
> From where shall my help come?
> My help comes from the LORD,
> Who made heaven and earth.
> He will not allow your foot to slip;
> He who keeps you will not slumber.
> Behold, He who keeps Israel
> Will neither slumber nor sleep.
> The LORD is your keeper;
> The LORD is your shade on your right hand.

The sun will not smite you by day,
Nor the moon by night.
The LORD will protect you from all evil;
He will keep your soul.
The LORD will guard your going out and your coming in
From this time forth and forever.

Psalm 121 (NASB)

While we look not at the things which are seen, but at the things which are not seen; for the things which are seen are temporal, but the things which are not seen are eternal.

2 Corinthians 4:18 (NASB)

Feeding Your Inner PK

There are things that we never want to let go of, people we never want to leave behind. But keep in mind that letting go isn't the end of the world, it's the beginning of a new life.

—Anonymous

Celebrate endings—for they precede new beginnings.

—Jonathan Lockwood Huie

Courage is the power to let go of the familiar.

—Raymond Lindquist

RICHARD M. SALAZAR JR.

Every exit is an entry somewhere.

—Tom Stoppard

Life is like riding a bicycle. To keep your balance you must keep moving.

—Albert Einstein

Some of us think holding on makes us strong, but sometimes it is letting go.

—Herman Hesse

Journal

What do I like *and* dislike about the community I live in?

_____

_____

_____

_____

_____

_____

_____

_____

_____

What activities does my community offer that I can participate in?

_____

_____

_____

_____

_____

_____

_____

_____

_____

What can I do right now to begin enjoying the community God has called me to?

_____

_____

_____

_____

_____

_____

_____

_____

_____

_____

Do I have a desire to see my community live for God? If not, why not?

_____

_____

_____

_____

_____

_____

RICHARD M. SALAZAR JR.

_____

_____

_____

_____

In what ways can God use me to represent Him to the people of my community?

_____

_____

_____

_____

_____

_____

_____

_____

_____

My prayer asking God to give me a peace and an enjoy-
ment within my community:

_____

_____

_____

_____

_____

_____

_____

_____

_____

Final Thought

As I pondered over the idea of adding a closing chapter, I couldn't think of anything worth saying that would make a lasting impact on your life other than a prayer. Think about what John said in 1 John 5:14-15, "And this is the confidence which we have before Him, that, if we ask anything according to His will, He hears us. And if we know that He hears us in whatever we ask, we know that we have the requests which we have asked from Him."

So it gives me great joy to spend my final thoughts asking God to grant His best for your life. Join me as I pray for you and your future!

Lord, I come to you praying for all of the sons
and daughters of pastors,
ministers, and missionaries who
open this book. I pray that
every time they use this tool to find answers
for their lives, that you would show yourself to be a
supernatural God
who takes great joy in showing each of them
unlimited love and favor. Send the
right kind of relationships
into their lives who will choose to express

unconditional love
and compassion for them and their future.
May they never
forget your promises, and as they
take their rightful
place in this life, may they always seek to
please no one else but you.
Amen.

Notes

Chapter 1 Notes:

_____

_____

_____

_____

_____

_____

_____

_____

_____

_____

_____

_____

_____

Chapter 2 Notes:

_____

_____

_____

_____

_____

_____

_____

_____

_____

_____

_____

_____

_____

Chapter 3 Notes:

_____

_____

_____

_____

_____

_____

_____

_____

_____

_____

_____

_____

_____

_____

Chapter 4 Notes:

_____

_____

_____

_____

_____

_____

_____

_____

_____

_____

_____

_____

_____

Chapter 5 Notes:

_____

_____

_____

_____

_____

_____

_____

_____

_____

_____

_____

_____

_____

Chapter 6 Notes:

_____

_____

_____

_____

_____

_____

_____

_____

_____

_____

_____

_____

_____

Chapter 7 Notes:

_____

_____

_____

_____

_____

_____

_____

_____

_____

_____

_____

_____

_____

Chapter 8 Notes:

_____

_____

_____

_____

_____

_____

_____

_____

_____

_____

_____

_____

_____

_____

Chapter 9 Notes:

Chapter 10 Notes:

_____

_____

_____

_____

_____

_____

_____

_____

_____

_____

_____

_____

_____

_____

Chapter 11 Notes:

_____

_____

_____

_____

_____

_____

_____

_____

_____

_____

_____

_____

_____

_____

Chapter 12 Notes:

_____

_____

_____

_____

_____

_____

_____

_____

_____

_____

_____

_____

_____

Chapter 13 Notes:

_____

_____

_____

_____

_____

_____

_____

_____

_____

_____

_____

_____

_____

Chapter 14 Notes:

_____

_____

_____

_____

_____

_____

_____

_____

_____

_____

_____

_____

_____

_____

Chapter 15 Notes:

_____

_____

_____

_____

_____

_____

_____

_____

_____

_____

_____

_____

_____

_____

References

Bakker, J., & Edlund, M. (2011). Fall to Grace. New York, NY, USA: Jericho Books.

Blake, I. C. (2010, July). Pastor for Life. *Ministry International* .

Hetzendorfer, R. (n.d.). Assessing the Positive Attributes of Preachers' Kids. *The Enrichment Journal* .